CITY SECRETS

City on Ice

Matt Sims

high noon books

City Secrets: *City on Ice*
Sound Out Level 5

> Each book in the Sound Out series is written in chapter format and gives students continued opportunities to practice decoding skills. Level 5 focuses on contractions, one-syllable spelling patterns, tense endings, and compound words.

Editor: Deb Akers
Book Design: Book Buddy Media

High Noon Books
a division of Academic Therapy Publications
20 Leveroni Court
Novato, CA 94949

Copyright 2009, 2018 by High Noon Books. All rights reserved. Printed in the United States of America. No part of this publication may be reproduced, stored in a retrieval system, or transmitted, in any form or by any means, electronic, mechanical photocopying, recording or otherwise, without the prior written permission of the publisher.

Images sourced from—
Getty Images: cover, pp. 3, 6, 7, 18, 24; Wikimedia/Public Domain: cover, pp. 10, 14, 16; Flickr/Eli Duke: p. 1; Shutterstock: pp. 4, 5, 8, 19; Wikimedia/U.S. Navy: p. 13; Newscom/ZUMA Press: pp. 20, 21, 28, 31; Newscom: p. 23; Newscom/William Sutton: p. 27; Pixabay: background

International Standard Book Number: 978-1-63402-229-3

29 28 27 26 25 24 23 22 21
12 11 10 09 08 07 06 05 04

HighNoonBooks.com

Set Order #2234-7

Contents

The Ice 5

Mac 11

A Place to Learn 15

A Day in the Life 19

Work and Play Hard 25

Hopes and Dreams 29

Atlantic Ocean
Pacific Ocean
Pacific Ocean
Indian Ocean
McMurdo Base

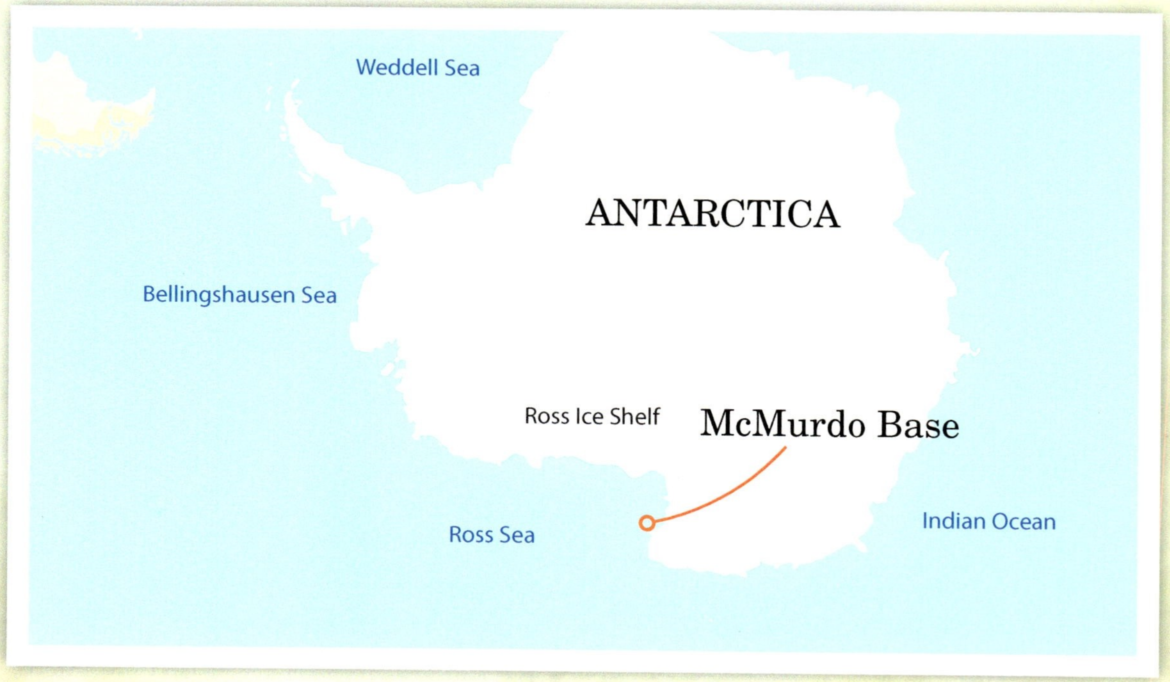
Weddell Sea
ANTARCTICA
Bellingshausen Sea
Ross Ice Shelf
McMurdo Base
Ross Sea
Indian Ocean

The Ice

The South Pole is the coldest place on Earth. No trees grow there. Big sheets of ice stretch over the land. That ice can be three miles thick.

The South Pole can get as cold as −100°. The winds blow at 200 miles an hour. People call this place the Ice.

The Ross Ice Shelf

Many sea birds and seals live around the South Pole. They fish for food. The seals have fat and fur that keep them warm.

People have a much harder time on the Ice.

We do not have enough hair to keep us warm. We often do not have much fat on us. It is easy for people to freeze when it is cold.

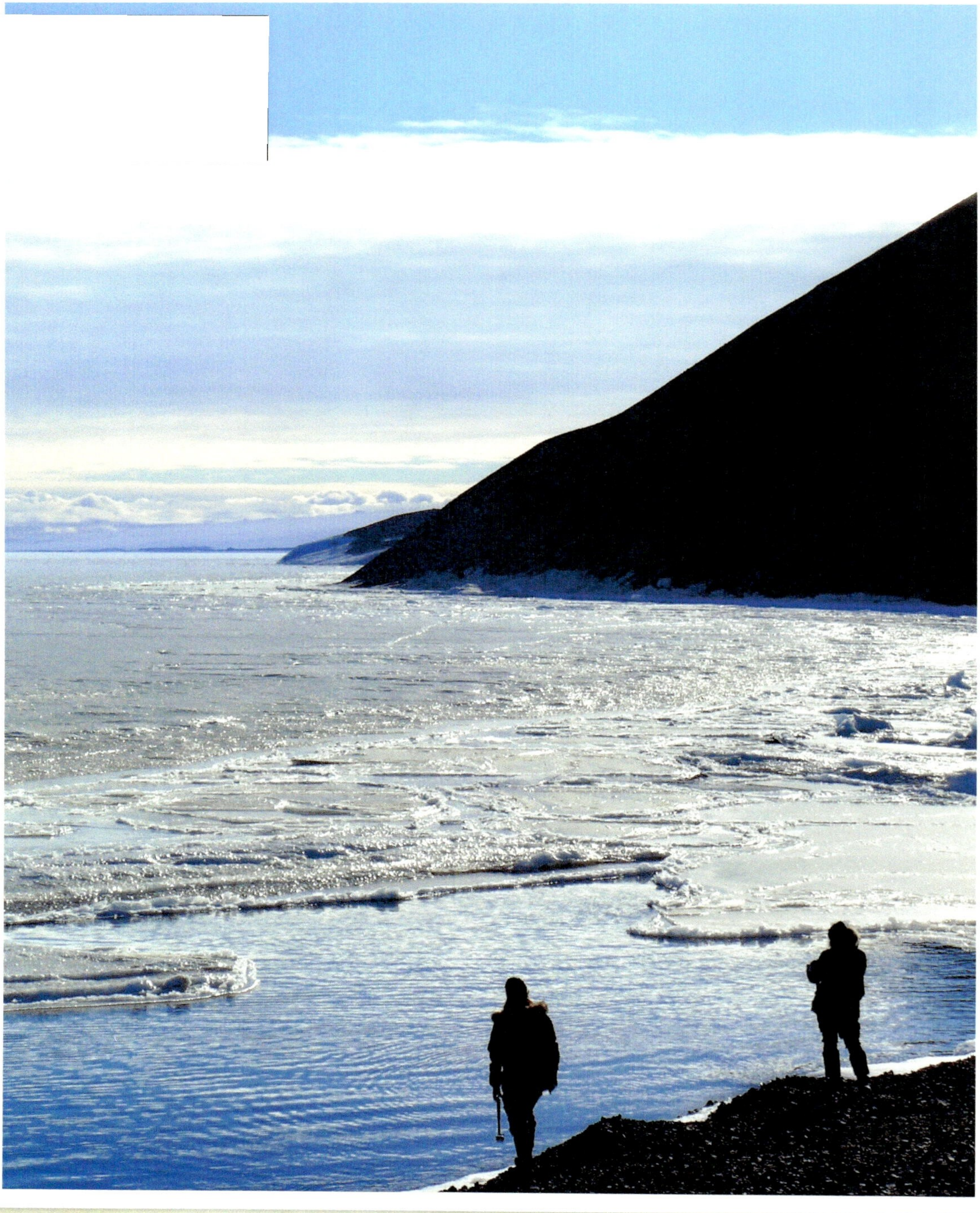

Why would anyone want to live at the South Pole? The truth is, the Ice is not a good place for most people. It takes someone who can brave the cold and wind of the South Pole.

There are people who dream of living at the South Pole. They train to be strong enough to live in the cold. There is a place for these people at the South Pole. It is a small city on the Ice.

Ross
Ice
Shelf

McMurdo Station

Ross Island

Scott Coast

Mac

Many people want to learn about the South Pole. Only some of them get to go there. McMurdo Base was built as a place for people to study the South Pole. People call the place "Mac" for short.

The Mac base is the largest town at the South Pole. It is built on a large, bare rock. At first, it was just a few huts and buildings. Now the Mac base has 100 buildings.

There are only two ways to get to the

Mac. There is an air strip close by. But planes can only land when the skies are clear. That is only a few months of the year!

The Mac base is right by the sea. Each year, a boat called the *Green Wave* comes to the base. The *Green Wave* has food and other things for people at the base. But first, it has to break through the sea ice.

A Coast Guard ship called the *Polar Star* carves a path through the ice. Then the *Green Wave* lands at the base. Sometimes, the ship cannot make it

The *Green Wave* at the base

through. Then the people at Mac have to thaw hot dogs from the freezer to eat!

Scott in his hut

A Place to Learn

The first man to live on the Ice was named Scott. He and his crew came to the South Pole on a ship. They spent six cold months at the South Pole.

Scott built a hut to live in. But the hut was not built well. It was drafty and very, very cold. The crew gave up and went back to their ship.

But the ship would not move. It was stuck in the ice! Scott and his crew had to camp out for many cold months on their boat.

The crew went out on short trips to look at the land of the South Pole. What they saw made them want to know more about this strange place.

Today, as many as 1,000 people live at the Mac base. They are there to learn about the South Pole. They hike out and watch sea birds and seals. They cross ice fields and climb steep cliffs. They pick up chunks of rock or ice. They take the pieces back to the base.

The base has labs where people look at what they have found. This is a great way to learn more about life at the South Pole.

View of Mac base

A Day in the Life

In some ways, the Mac base is like any other city. There are lights. There are pipes for water. There are phones. Since the base is built on rock, all of these lines and pipes run above ground.

Pipes above ground

The base has a place to check out books. There is also a fire house with trucks. There is a place to go if you get sick. You can even go bowling if you want!

But the Mac base is not like any other city. People have to spend a lot of time inside. Even in summer, the South Pole is only 30°. There are 18 hours of sun light. But in winter, you hardly see the sun at all.

Winter is the best time to see the Southern Lights.

There are few plants and no trees at the South Pole. The people miss seeing green plants. So they built a green house on the Mac base.

Now people can grow things to eat. But they mostly like to come and sit in the green house. They like to look at the bright green leaves of the plants. They like feeling the moist, soft air. It helps them feel like they are still on Earth, and not the moon!

Relaxing in a hammock in the Mac green house

23

Taking a hike near the base

Work and Play Hard

Life on the Mac base can be hard. People work ten hours a day. They work six days a week.

People do get outside the base and go on hikes. But the land around the Mac base is full of ice holes. A hiker could fall in a hole. Hikers have to tell the others when they will be back. If they are not back in time, a crew goes out to search.

Some say the hardest part of living at

the Mac base is finding a way to have fun! When it is time to play, there is not much to do. So the Mac staff makes their own fun.

One fun thing is the Ice Run. People race to the icy sea. Then they jump in the sea in their swim suits!

Is it ever cold! Then the group gets in a big hot tub. The Mac staff plans these kinds of fun things each year. It helps them get through the long, cold months.

Start of the Ice Run

28

Hopes and Dreams

The Mac staff tries to make sure that they do not hurt the land around the South Pole.

People try to reuse things. They leave no trash on the base.

Someone had the thought of getting dirt bikes to ride around the base. Bikes do not mess up the air like trucks. Now many people ride bikes at the Mac base.

Life at the South Pole can teach us about how the Earth works.

In past years, the Mac staff has

watched the ice cap at the South Pole. That ice is melting. This is very bad news for people. If the ice keeps melting, the sea will get higher. Life on Earth will not be the same.

The staff at Mac base hopes to teach people to take care of the Earth. Their dream is a clean, safe Earth for all living things.

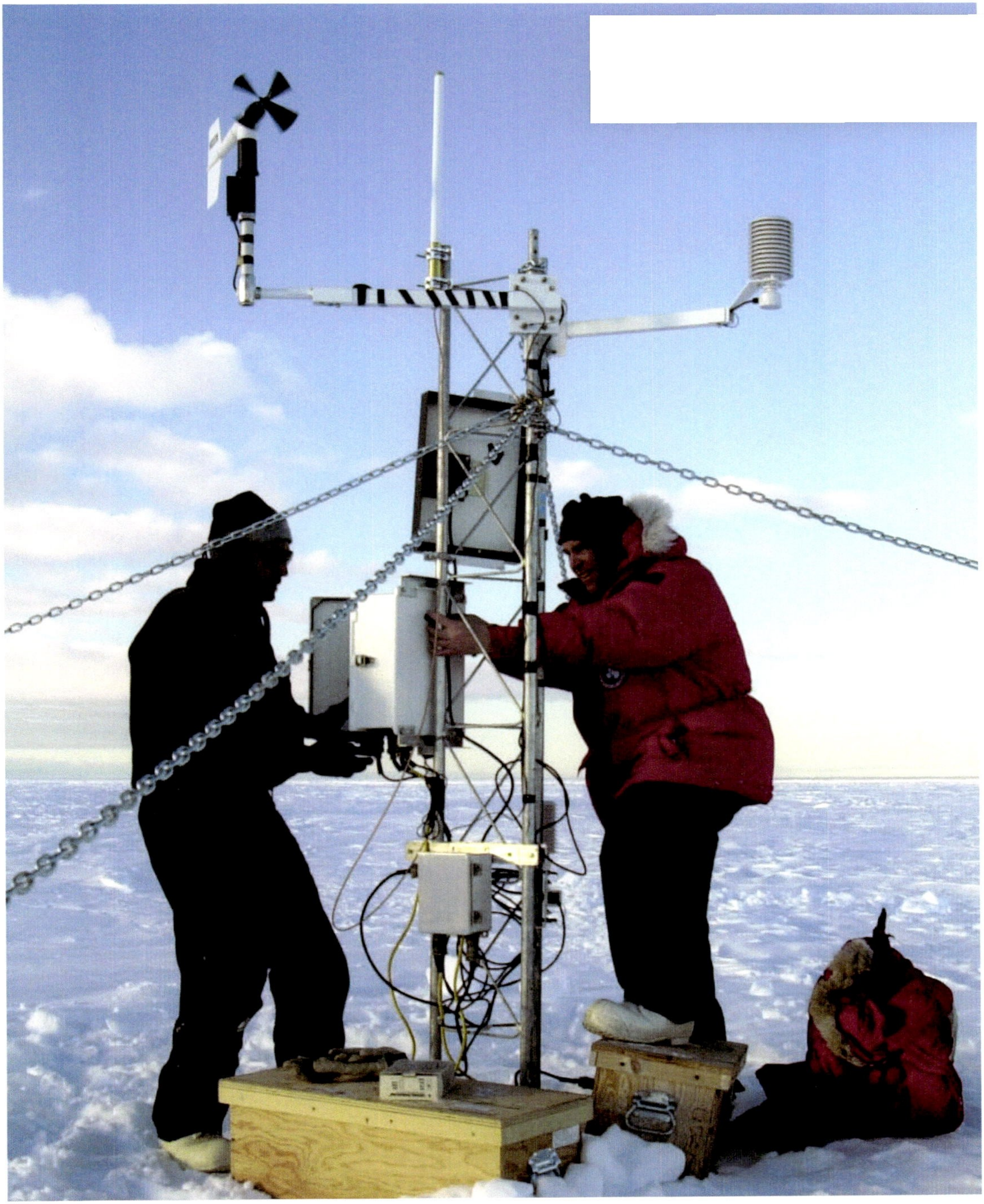

High Frequency Words

an	is	there
and	it	they
around	just	this
as	live	three
be	many	two
call	no	us
can	of	want
do	on	was
for	over	we
get	that	who
good	the	why
have	them	would